Access to Online Resources

Kristina Botyriute

Access to Online Resources

A Guide for the Modern Librarian

Springer Open

Kristina Botyriute
Open Athens, Eduserv
Bath, UK

Photographs by Danielle Mac Innes, Edward Borton, Phil Coffman, Kristina Botyriute, Kai Oberhäuser, Pavan Trikutam, Angelika Levshakova, Philipp Berndt, Antonina Bukowska, Riciardus, Jakob Owens, Margarida C Silva, Clem Onojeghuo, Michał Parzuchowski, Daria Nepriakhina, Anastasia Petrova, Antonio Lapa, Tim Gouw, Marc Wieland, rawpixel.com, Jessica Furtney, David Marcu and Hand drawn illustrations by Ieva Botyriute

ISBN 978-3-319-73989-2   ISBN 978-3-319-73990-8   (eBook)
https://doi.org/10.1007/978-3-319-73990-8

Library of Congress Control Number: 2018935111

© The Editor(s) (if applicable) and The Author(s) 2018. This book is an open access publication.
Open Access This book is licensed under the terms of the Creative Commons Attribution 4.0 International License (http://creativecommons.org/licenses/by/4.0/), which permits use, sharing, adaptation, distribution and reproduction in any medium or format, as long as you give appropriate credit to the original author(s) and the source, provide a link to the Creative Commons license and indicate if changes were made.
The images or other third party material in this book are included in the book's Creative Commons license, unless indicated otherwise in a credit line to the material. If material is not included in the book's Creative Commons license and your intended use is not permitted by statutory regulation or exceeds the permitted use, you will need to obtain permission directly from the copyright holder.
The use of general descriptive names, registered names, trademarks, service marks, etc. in this publication does not imply, even in the absence of a specific statement, that such names are exempt from the relevant protective laws and regulations and therefore free for general use.
The publisher, the authors and the editors are safe to assume that the advice and information in this book are believed to be true and accurate at the date of publication. Neither the publisher nor the authors or the editors give a warranty, express or implied, with respect to the material contained herein or for any errors or omissions that may have been made. The publisher remains neutral with regard to jurisdictional claims in published maps and institutional affiliations.

Cover Illustration: Front cover photograph by Ashley Batz: Back cover photograph by Jill Heyer

Printed and bound by CPI Group (UK) Ltd, Croydon, CR0 4YY on acid-free paper

This Springer imprint is published by the registered company Springer International Publishing AG part of Springer Nature.
The registered company address is: Gewerbestrasse 11, 6330 Cham, Switzerland

Helping you get the most out of life by helping you get the most out of technology.

Eduserv

TABLE OF CONTENTS

01 Introduction

02 Authentication and Authorisation
Jane and Ben
Before we start...

03 Web based authentication
What is HTTP?
HTTP Basic Authentication
HTTP Digest Authentication
HTTP(S) Forms Authentication
Cookies!
More about cookies...
King and bishop: certificates
Key concepts

04 IP address recognition
On and off site
Remote access: local build vs cloud based
Security considerations
Key concepts

05 SAML
How it works
You...
...and Them
Federation
Key concepts

06 OpenID Connect
Open Authorisation 2.0
OpenID Connect
Key concepts

07 Basic Troubleshooting
60 second diagnostics
Setting up access
The fastest way to get help
The End
Bibliography

Introduction

"Access management is a very complicated beast", concluded one of my customers at the end of a lengthy support call. This might indeed reflect how many librarians feel these days but it doesn't need to be! After reading this book, you will be able to skillfully navigate the maze of online access management technologies and decide what serves your library's needs best.

According to Gartner IT Glossary (2012), "identity and access management (IAM) is the security discipline that enabled the right individuals to access the right resources at the right times for the right reasons." Simply put, it is making sure your users are who they say they are and only have access to what you want them to have access to. In addition to preventing unauthorised parties from exploiting your organisation's resources, IAM technologies can help manage subscriptions to online resources where cost is based on the number of users accessing protected content.

Some publishers charge for every single user, in which case you will want to make sure you have an up-to-date list of individuals who need this resource as well as ensure appropriate permissions are in place. This is particularly relevant to small libraries where the budget is limited.

As an international technical pre-sales consultant for OpenAthens, I frequently speak to librarians from all over the world. The sheer number of technologies a typical librarian deals with on a daily basis is astonishing. Often they are expected to learn-on-the-job, which can be stressful in a busy environment especially if communication between the library and IT department is poor.

The following chapters are written for knowledge workers who are involved with managing access to digital content online and cannot afford the time to read book after book of technical material to make sense of all the nuts and bolts that make up the IAM. I have covered all the main concepts in this book.

Authentication and Authorisation

02

Jane and Ben

Monday morning. Electronic resources librarian Jane makes herself a cup of coffee, sits down at her desk and types in her username and password into the login screen. Instantly, the computer sends these credentials to a central place - the directory, where all organisational accounts are listed. The most popular of these is Microsoft's Active Directory but on a rare occasion you may be dealing with alternatives such as OpenLDAP, Univentions (UCS), ApacheDS or even the futuristic concept of Directory-as-a-Service.

So what happens when Jane's credentials reach the directory? The server checks if Jane is a registered user and if the password is correct. If so, she is authenticated into the system.

Jane opens the shared drive to find some reports but accidentally clicks on the 'HR' icon, causing a warning message to appear advising she does not have permission to access to this folder. She then clicks on the 'Reports' as initially intended and it opens. This is an authorisation decision influenced by a variety of security policies in Jane's organisation, determining specific permissions for each user or user group.

In the context of accessing digital resources online, authentication and authorisation may occur a number of times before users are presented with the content they are trying to access.

Ben is a chemistry student who has found an interesting article on ScienceDirect (sciencedirect.com). In order to read full article, Ben must sign into the website. He knows his university has access to content on this website and selects the 'Sign in via your Institution' option. The following sequence of events may sound like a long intricate process but in reality it gets executed in a split second:

First, a form for credentials is displayed and as soon as Ben enters his details, his organisation authenticates him as a valid user.

Then, Ben's institution passes a small set of information to ScienceDirect. This set includes details about Ben as well as his university and is used by the publisher to carry out authentication against the list of subscribing organisations. We can think of it as a second round of the same process, only now on provider's end.

Lastly, university is verified to have a valid subscription and authentication is successful, however the article of interest is published in a journal his institution has not yet bought the access to and the authorisation fails.

Ben sets off to his university's library to discuss his options...

☞ KEY POINTS

Authentication validates user's identity. Who are you?   **Authorisation** checks what permissions the user has. What can you access?

Before we start...

Before we go ahead, we need to make friends with one concept. A PROTOCOL is a big scary word, often used by IT guys to scare people off so they don't have to work as much (I am joking, of course). My personal, if somewhat geeky, opinion is that everything boils down to a protocol. I will explain.

A Shopping Protocol. ASP.

One must walk into a shop, collect items into a trolley or a shopping basket and either self-checkout or go to the till to pay. Whilst there may be variation in customers' choice of items' container and the method of checkout, ultimately the procedure is to collect items, pay and leave. Any other way to obtain goods from the shop is non-standard and usually unsupported by law.

Essentially, a protocol is a set of rules designed to make our life easier. The sequence of events may vary in length and execution depending on who is doing the shopping but the rules of the protocol enable a clear goal, path and outcome.

What about online shopping? Well, this would be ASP 2.0 Important thing to note though is that a higher version of something does not always guarantee an improvement - sometimes it is just another way of achieving the same result.

With that in mind, let's go ahead and explore the most common authentication and authorisation methods that protect the digital content online today.

Web based authentication methods

What is HTTP?

HTTP stands for Hyper Text Transfer Protocol.
It is a set of rules of transferring files on the World Wide Web. When you open your browser and type in an address, you are really saying: 'GET me this web page!'. Collaborating with a number of other protocols, HTTP fetches you the page and serves it up on the screen.

GET https://www.google.com/search?q=**test**

Requesting information is not the only thing you can do with this useful protocol. Whilst there is no need to explore all nine methods of HTTP, we will look at another popular one - POST. What does it do? Exactly what it says - it allows you to send information. The link in your browser is the address on an envelope and the 'letter' with information is enclosed within.

POST https://www.any_internet_store.com/Login

logonID: username
logonPassword: password

Web based authentication has many flavours and what we know as 'username and password' uses three of them:

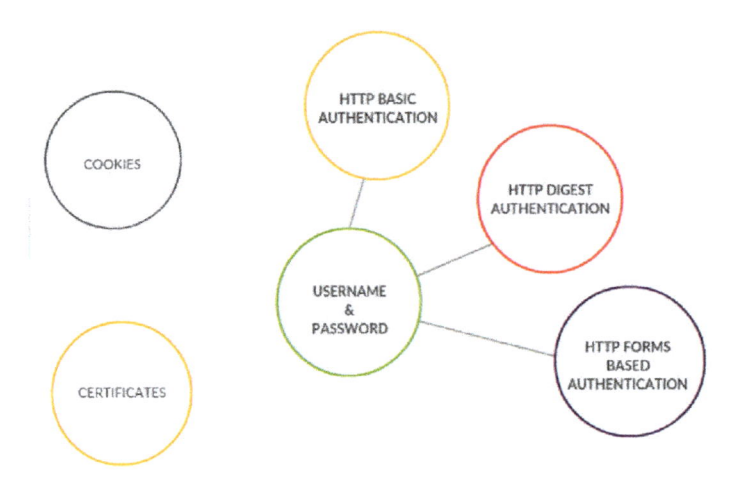

- COOKIES
- HTTP BASIC AUTHENTICATION
- HTTP DIGEST AUTHENTICATION
- USERNAME & PASSWORD
- HTTP FORMS BASED AUTHENTICATION
- CERTIFICATES

There is a lot more to this simple method than meets the eye and we will delve right into what happens behind the scenes.

👉 KEY POINTS

Hyper Text Transfer Protocol (HTTP) facilitates communication of data on the World Wide Web

GET is a way to request data

POST is a way to submit data

HTTP Basic Authentication

HTTP Basic Authentication is the oldest username and password authentication method there is. It dates back to 1989, when Sir Tim Berners-Lee invented the World Wide Web. It works like this: a user types in credentials and from then on they must be passed to the website each time the user's actions result in a request for any new content to be displayed. Remember GET? This is it! When content is protected by Basic Authentication whenever the user clicks to open a new article, types in a search query or navigates to a different area of the website credentials will have to be included in that request. Here is how this might look like:

http://**username:password**@www.example.com
http://example.com?un=**username**&psw=**password**

This could get quite inconvenient if one was forced to type their username and password over and over again. Instead of prompting for login every other click, the web browser takes care of this by helpfully storing user's credentials until a logout button gets hit or the web browser window is closed.

Needless to say, due to it's age HTTP Basic Authentication has major security flaws. As you have already noticed, the example links on the left are passing the username and password in clear text.
This authentication method supports base64 encoding too but it doesn't make it more secure as the text can be decoded in seconds using online tools. Can you guess what is encoded in this link?

https://example.com?un=**dXNlcm5hbWU=**&psw=**cGFzc3dvcmQ=**

(If you can't, go to base64decode.org and copy-paste the values in bold.)
Although most digital publishers opt for more secure methods to protect their content, some still support Basic Authentication. Reasons range from scarce development resources to faith in humanity.
Fortunately for us, this method has a distinct pop-up login screen which will help you identify it - see next page for a real life example. Whilst I am not advocating the idea, I have seen institutions negotiate lower subscription prices upon discovery of Basic Auth. Others have effectively encouraged their provider into implementing an alternative authentication method.

HTTP Digest Authentication

This is a more secure version of HTTP Basic Authentication. From user's perspective everything looks the same (real life example of BA, as promised):

The only difference with Digest Authentication is that the password will no longer be sent in clear or base64 encoded text. It is now encoded and hashed. What is a hash? Otherwise known as a message digest, a hash is a value representing the original string. For example: 'password' hashed in MD5 is '5f4dcc3b5aa765d61d8327deb882cf99'

MD5 (Message Digest 5) is the default algorithm used for HTTP Digest Authentication. Problem? MD5 can be cracked in a blink. hashkiller.co.uk cracked the above example in 104 milliseconds.

Upon a (hopefully brief) encounter with Digest Authentication, my best advice is to note what the creators themselves said about the method:

"The Digest Access Authentication scheme is not intended to be a complete answer to the need for security in the World Wide Web. This scheme provides no encryption of message content. The intent is simply to create an access authentication method that avoids the most serious flaws of Basic Authentication." (Leach et al., 1999)

KEY POINTS

HTTP Basic Authentication passes credentials within the link, in clear or base64 encoded text

HTTP Digest Authentication hashes the password with MD5

base64 can be decoded using tools freely available online

MD5 is the default algorithm used for HTTP DA. This algorithm was first cracked in 1996 and considered unsuitable for use since 2010

HTTP(S) Forms Authentication

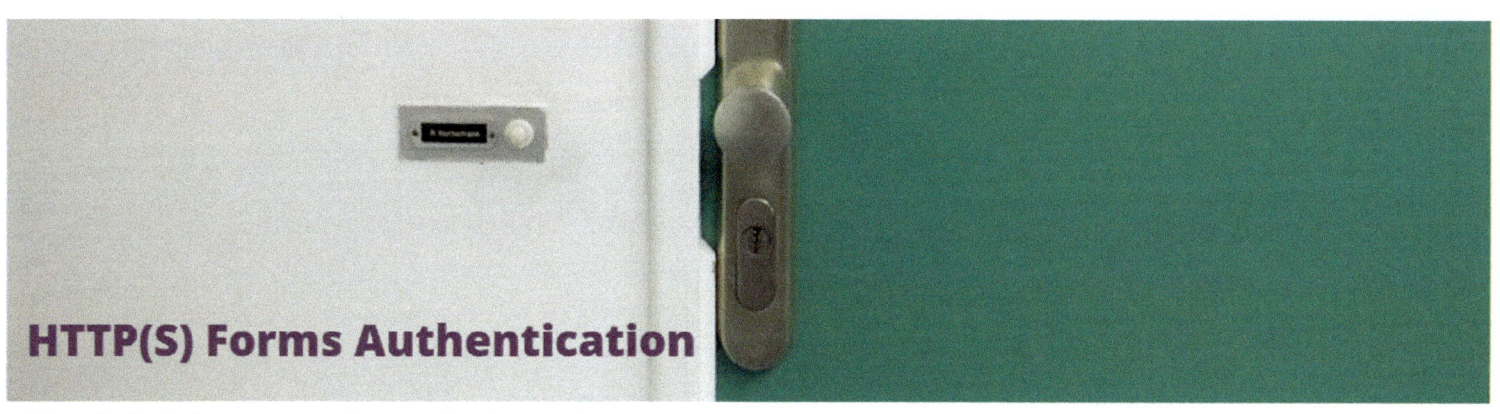

This method submits username and password to the server by power of POST. (Think of an envelope with a letter inside). It does so in clear text, however it is most commonly used with HTTPS for added security. (Think of an envelope with a magic seal on top).

What is HTTPS? Hyper Text Transfer Protocol Secure. You know it's in use when you see this: 🔒 Secure https://

Forms authentication is incredibly popular and is the most widely adopted variant of username and password authentication.

POST as a method is more secure than GET: it will never pass data in the address bar, it will not be cached or remain in the browser history. Still, it can be read if intercepted unless used in conjunction with HTTPS. To illustrate the process, I will attempt to access MAG Online Library. POST to: https://www.magonlinelibrary.com/action/doLogin

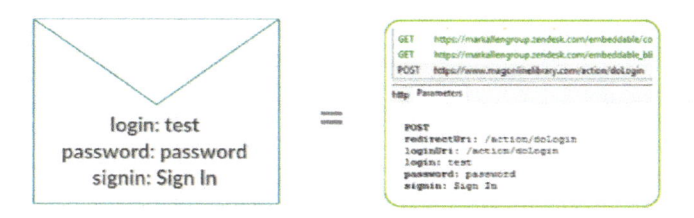

Username and Password do not match.

The result is an error message, as expected. Should my credentials have matched the records on publisher's end, the code on the website would have changed to contain my username and password in the login form. This would then be used to redirect me to the post-login screen, print 'Hello, Test' and potentially load my personal profile for this website.

HTTPS forms authentication is a much better way to connect individual users to protected content than Basic or Digest Authentication. For one, the login form will look and behave as desired by the creator whilst the other two leave us stuck with a pop-up box and an ugly error 401 when things go south. Many publishers support forms authentication as an option for individual subscribers whilst institutional users are often encouraged to use federated access, covered later in this book.

> 👉 **KEY POINTS**
>
> **POST https://www.example.com/auth.php** - more secure than GET but data can be read if intercepted by man in the middle attack
>
> **POST https://www.example.com/auth.php** - most secure: credentials are encoded and therefore useless if captured.

11

Cookies!

"By continuing to use this site you consent to the use of cookies on your device as described in our cookie policy unless you have disabled them. You can change your cookie settings at any time but parts of our site will not function correctly without them" (ft.com)

Also known as HTTP entity authentication, cookies are different from username and password driven recognition. Much like real cookies, digital ones also enhance the quality of life - or in particular, user experience on the web. As I'm sure you will agree, we would struggle to find a website that does not make use of cookies in this day and age. So, what is this cookie?

A cookie is a small piece of text that stores information about your interaction with a website. If you clicked on the cookie policy hyperlink in the notification displayed at the top of this page, you would have been taken to one of the nicest cookie policy explanation pages I've come across so far. Not all publishers go into trouble of explaining themselves in such detail and therefore it is worth familiarising with how cookies work. According to Wright, Freedman and Liu (2008) "in contradiction to the claim that no information is sent from your computer to anybody outside your system, the majority of cookies are interactive (that is, the information is not only written to them but also read from them by the web servers you connect to)."

Session cookies will 'go out of date' as soon as the browser is closed or the session time is up. This means that if my aunt Mary was shopping for groceries for her Sunday roast and had a cart full of goodies, one unfortunate click on the red X at the top of the browser would render her cart empty when she navigates back to the site. Such an event would likely cause her some grief and perhaps this is one of the reasons why session cookies are not overly popular amongst online retailers. What if the browser was set to purposely deny session cookies? My aunt Mary would not be able to add any potatoes to her cart at all! Websites do not have a memory of their own and so she would be treated as a new visitor every time she opened a different page.

Persistent cookies are either stored in "jars" on your browser or on your device, in the hard drive. Being plain strings of text they cannot do anything on their own but are detectable by websites and serve as reminders of the visitor's language preference, bookmarks or theme selection. On rare occasions cookies would store user's credentials which could result in auto-login although from a security perspective this is not something that should be endorsed.

> **KEY POINT**
> **Cookies come in two flavours: persistent and session**

More about cookies...

When a cookie is initially set, several very important parameters are specified: cookie's name, expiry date, domain, session identifier and path.

NAME: Chocolate Chip Cookie
EXPIRY DATE: 03/2020
BRAND: Cookie Company
SESSION: first shopping today
PATH: 3rd isle from the left

There are others, such as a **secure** parameter, but they aren't always used. Let's take a look at how the cookie is set upon clicking 'Accept and Close' when visiting nature.com:

⚠ We use cookies to improve your experience with our site.   Accept and close | More info.

```
POST
cookies: accepted
Set-Cookie: euCookieNotice=accepted; domain=www.nature.com;
path=/; expires=Mon, 02 Jul 2018 16:31:07 -0000; HttpOnly
```

Looks technical? Here's what it all means.

euCookieNotice=accepted; acknowledges my acceptance of cookies
domain=www.nature.com; means the cookie will only be valid here
If nature.com had any sub-domains, such as '**xyz**.nature.com' then a separate cookie would have to be set for those
How would we set a cookie to include all sub-domains? '**.nature.com**'
path=/; means the cookie will apply to all pages on this domain, not just this particular one
expires=Mon, 02 Jul 2018 16:31:07 -0000; sets cookie's lifetime to a year

As you will have already noticed, there is no session identifier. This means the cookie we've just analysed is not a session one. To check, simply close the browser and re-open again - did you see the cookie message appear at the top? Just for fun, I checked what else was set on my browser as soon as I got to the website. The list turned out to be quite extensive, containing both session and persistent cookies (yes, all of those folders, not just nature.com):

Site	Cookie Name
doubleclick.net	
imrworldwide.com	
kxcd.net	
nature.com	
scorecardresearch.com	
springernature.com	
statse.webtrendslive.com	

☞ **KEY POINTS**

Cookies can significantly enhance user experience and some use of them is essential. Presenting users with a message that signifies acceptance of all cookies on the site is required by law in many countries.

Clear your cache and cookies if bothered by unsolicited ads (or install an advert blocking extension).

Check the cookie policy if not presented with informational message - it is good fun and good practice to know who is interested in your activity online

King and bishop: certificates

I am yet to see an online content publisher who would insist on this form of authentication. It is useful to know nevertheless as you may be using certificates to access Office 365, protect connection to your work network over the VPN or even just log into the portal where all of your digital resources are listed. Certificate authentication can replace user credentials or be used in conjunction for increased security. Winnard et al. (2016) defined the concept in the following way: "one party uses a certificate to identify itself, the other party must validate it. This process is referred to as a handshake."

At the risk of sounding medieval when explaining modern technology, I will compare a digital certificate to an official seal, confirming to the King the letter is from the bishop. The bishop will have used his ring to stamp it, then ordered his trusted messenger to deliver the letter to the King. This letter is of high importance and the King needs to be certain that the seal is not forged. What if someone has stolen the bishop's ring and went on stamping about? He refers the matter to the archbishop (Certificate Authority) - a highly respected and trusted individual who is in charge of and regularly keeps in touch with all the bishops. The archbishop inspects the seal and confirms it's validity. He also informs the King the sender is alive and well, as he has only recently attended a dinner party with him.

The King is now sufficiently assured of the authenticity of this letter and proceeds to read it.

Suppose the bishop has been demoted - he would then be added to the revocation list and the archbishop would advise the King to not trust any correspondence sealed with the demoted bishop's stamp.
The same would apply if the bishop's reign in the region has come to an end (this would unfortunately mean the bishop has passed away) - the archbishop would notify the King the official seal has expired and should not be trusted.

When you are a King, here is how your browser would declare it:

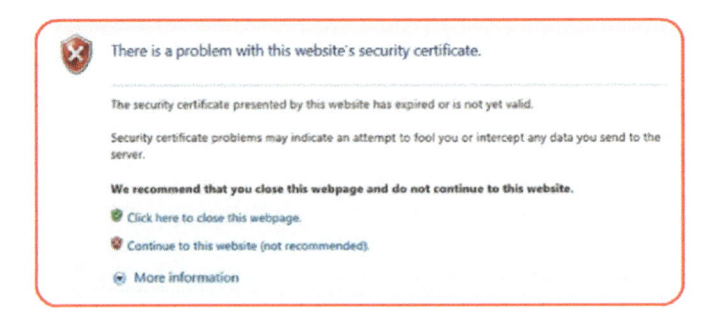

> **There is a problem with this website's security certificate.**
>
> The security certificate presented by this website has expired or is not yet valid.
>
> Security certificate problems may indicate an attempt to fool you or intercept any data you send to the server.
>
> **We recommend that you close this webpage and do not continue to this website.**
>
> 🟢 Click here to close this webpage.
>
> 🔴 Continue to this website (not recommended).
>
> ⊙ More information

Key concepts

HTTP
Facilitates data exchange on the WWW. Uses GET to fetch information and POST to send it

BASIC AUTHENTICATION
Passes user credentials in the URL in plain or base64 encoded text

DIGEST AUTHENTICATION
Passes MD5 hashed user credentials in the URL

FORMS AUTHENTICATION
Submits user credentials directly into the code

COOKIES
Used to enhance user experience, can be persistent or session

CERTIFICATES
Helps confirm authenticity and trustworthiness of digital entities

IP Recognition

On and off site

IP address recognition, often referred to as a "traditional authentication method", is very old. It pre-dates the HTTP Basic Authentication discussed earlier on and goes as far back as 1970s - the time before the World Wide Web as we know it. Why did I call it recognition, not authentication? Because the elements required to identify an individual are missing. It deals with **authorisation only** and works by checking whether the traffic is coming from a known location. For example: Ray wants to access the International Journal of Metrology and Quality Engineering. His institution subscribes to it and Ray is accessing from an on-campus computer. Upon detecting a new connection, metrology-journal.org checks Ray's IP address against the list of authorised IP addresses and grants access to the content.

IP recognition is without a doubt the most widely used method for institutional logins in the online publishing industry. This is a very convenient option that requires minimal effort to set up - a simple network firewall can do the job. Here is another common scenario: a university is purchasing subscription to an online resource, such as Annals of Internal Medicine. The range of university's IP addresses is specified on the order form, the publisher adds them into the entitlements' system (or a firewall access list) and job done!

The traffic for each incoming IP is likely to be monitored for security reasons and to measure usage which may influence the cost when it comes to renewal. The setup itself though is exceptionally straightforward. But how do we use the same method to enable access for users off-site?

The reigning king of IP-based remote access technologies is a proxy server. Let's use a medical student, Helen, to illustrate how this works. The deadline is fast approaching and Helen needs to access annals.org from home to complete her assignment. She logs into the library portal where links to various online resources are listed and clicks on 'Annals of Internal Medicine' link which is configured to route the request via her university's proxy server. The proxy changes Helen's IP address into one that has been pre-agreed to represent this institution and the publisher authorises access based on the proxy IP instead of Helen's real one.

Remote access via proxy: local build vs cloud based

Some organisations like to keep it all in-house, in particular those benefiting from a large IT team or those that do not believe in cloud technologies. A proxy server is either installed as a stand-alone entity on the local network or may come as an add-on feature of another IAM technology, such as OpenAthens LA. In such a setup, the organisation takes full responsibility for the maintenance of it's own proxy server - patching, upgrades, resilient architecture, everything. When strict security policies must be adhered to but the institution still wishes to utilise IP recognition for remote access this is often a good choice. Some providers charge per traffic volume or limit number of concurrent sessions. In response to that, some IT teams feel that having a proxy server on-site helps them maintain a better grip on usage management. EZProxy is an example of a proxy well-known to academic libraries. It offers two options - locally installed EZProxy server or Online Computer Library Center (OCLC) hosted service. Whilst ideas to create an open source alternative are surfacing due to the observed continuous rise in prices for this service (Sabol, 2016), the only real alternatives today are Web Access Management (WAM) proxy or OpenAthens, where a managed proxy service is part of the package.

Hosted proxy services take a lot of stress away as the provider takes care of all the upgrades, maintenance and guarantees a high uptime of the service. As with everything, migration from a local installation to hosted service requires careful planning. Lynne Edgar from Texas Tech University (TTU) libraries (2015) has shared the experience of migration in the Journal of Electronic Resources Librarianship, making the following recommendation: "I suggest other libraries thoroughly understand their authentication process <...> when implementing a hosted service. <...> Be sure to ascertain the process used to access resources via mobile devices when moving to hosted EZProxy. Ensure tablets and phones will be able to access all of your electronic resources formats whether users are on or off campus".

Her recommendation to thoroughly understand local authentication process is sound and applicable whichever IAM solution you may be considering. If you know what systems are in place and what your user journey looks like, a good support team should be able to assist you with the rest. In TTU Libraries' case, the process of migration has unintentionally stretched out to seven months and there was a loss of service to external patrons along the way.

KEY POINTS

A locally hosted proxy server will have to be looked after. Organisations that have implemented this solution commonly have a dedicated member of staff who continuously updates proxy configurations.

Proxy in the cloud takes a lot of work off your hands and is much more convenient than a locally hosted one. Understanding of your institution's security policies as well as existing user journey will help reduce disruptions during the implementation.

"On average, 58% of the IP ranges held by publishers to authenticate libraries who license their content are inaccurate"

———

PUBLISHER SOLUTIONS INTERNATIONAL, 2017

Security considerations

As convenient as it may be, IP recognition has it's flaws. Many publishers code their websites in such a manner as to aid the researchers in their efforts. This aid would often take form of personalisation features, such as ability to save useful articles or advanced search queries, compile a list of references, share material with fellow researchers and so on. All of this convenience is unattainable when IP address is used for authorisation. Why? Because the IP address does not uniquely identify a user, unless the user has a static address configured on the device and that device is utilised exclusively by that one user which is a somewhat unlikely scenario. In fact, it is common practice to only use one or two IP addresses to identify the whole site! The most a digital content provider can achieve is match the incoming IP address to the list of subscribers and make a remark of this somewhere on the website, such as "This resource is provided to you courtesy of Helen's University".

Something to consider: networking teams rarely discuss their work with the library (nor would librarians find it interesting). So whenever institution's external IP address changes, the library would be informed of the new one and the old one would be left to function for a while to avoid any disruptions. How often do we bother to contact all the publishers to remove the old IP address? My experience shows this is not a common practice as many subscribers get misrecognized every other day and contact our service desk for help.

In addition to being susceptible to man-in-the-middle attacks, access by IP recognition has been discovered to suffer from general abuse by subscribers. Publisher Solutions International, Ltd (2017) have recently carried out an extensive research and data cleanup exercise where they have come across numerous instances of misuse and license abuse... This lead to opening of the ipregistry.org - a growing repository of approximately 1.5 billion validated IP addresses from over 60,000 organisations worldwide. These addresses are added and updated by subscribing institutions themselves, however the benefit is that they only have to do this once. Participating publishers are keeping an eye on this list and upon detecting changes on their subscribers' records, update their access management systems automatically.

The site has just gone live but has already been enthusiastically greeted by large publishers such as Wiley and Cambridge University Press as well as librarians in the hope they will be able to cut down on manual effort required to update every provider every time one of their on-site or proxy IP addresses change.

> **KEY POINT**
>
> IP recognition is easy to implement and is sometimes perceived as the key element to guarantee anonymity. It is also a trade-off between convenience for the library and convenience for the end user.

Key concepts

IP RECOGNITION
Authorisation based on the incoming IP address

PROXY
Aids remote access by presenting a pre-configured IP address to provider instead of the real one

REMOTE ACCESS
Access from outside of your institution

THEIPREGISRY.ORG
A site where institutions register their IP addresses used for on-site IP recognition

MAN-IN-THE-MIDDLE ATTACK
Eavesdropping. Interception of communication between two systems

SAML

23

"While it may seem like no one is paying attention, internet users are starting to realize their data has value. And it's a value that deserves better than a password."

———

JOHN FONTANA, 2017

How it works

Security Assertion Markup Language - SAML (sam-el) is a well-established and mature open standard, designed for the best possible user experience with the added benefit of maximum security. Praised by information security professionals, it passes selective information about an individual without ever giving out user's credentials! Better yet, one of the main purposes of this protocol is to aid Single Sign On which takes care of the headache associated with maintaining passwords. Sounds magical? Let's have a look at how it works.

An engineering student Ed wants to watch a video on the IET.tv website. To gain access, he needs to login via his institution or register as an individual subscriber and pay the fee. Ed selects the 'Federation Login' option, selects to login via UK Federation, picks his institution from the list. IET then forwards him to his unviersity's login page so he may authenticate himself. The username and password are accepted and the university replies directly to the publisher with requested information about this student, confirming he belongs to the institution and is entitled to access this resource. The publisher checks the response contains what they need to make an authorisation decision and if everything matches up - Ed is granted access to the video of his interest. Happy days!

Consider the following picture illustrating a similar scenario:

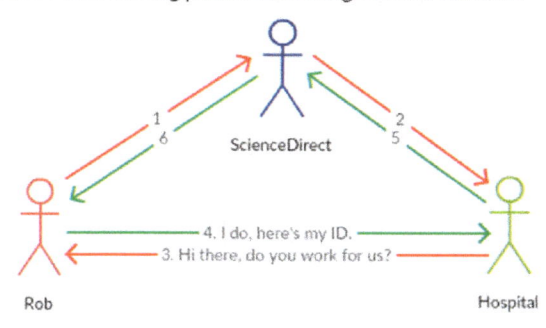

1. I want to read this article about stem cells. I'm from the Hospital.
2. Hospital, do you know this guy?
3. Hi there, do you work for us?
4. I do, here's my ID.
5. Ah yeah, that's Rob. He works for us.
6. Hi Rob, nice to meet you! Please proceed to read the article.

Although implementation of SAML requires a little more effort on publisher's end than HTTP Basic Authentication or IP recognition, it does pay for itself and is therefore becoming increasingly popular, especially where digital content is of high value. Giant publishing houses such as McGraw-Hill, Oxford University Press and Elsevier were among the first to adopt SAML authentication for institutional subscribers.

> ☞ **KEY POINT** SAML authentication does not expose users credentials, validating access based on the selective information passed in the background instead.

You...

The decision to trust someone is often made based on what you know about that person. Trust is the key principle of SAML and like in real life, identity plays a major part. Similar to a country issuing passports to it's citizens, you - as an institution - are providing virtual identities to your users. Depending on your security and data protection policies, you will be collecting certain information about them, such as name and surname, email address, position, maybe even home address, telephone number, date of birth and the shoe size! This helps create an accurate user profile, stamp it with a unique username and assign appropriate permissions and privileges for each individual. In the world of SAML, your country is called an IdP - Identity Provider. This is very important! The identity provider is you.

Now that you have a country to rule, you need a country code. Whilst you would expect one to three digits in a normal world, Identity Providers are defined by a unique string of characters that often look like a web address but isn't (just to confuse you). It's called an entityID. For example: "https://idp.adamscollege.edu/entity" might identify Adams College. An important thing to remember is that it doesn't do anything - if you clicked on it, it wouldn't take you anywhere.
So why the weird notation? Well...for one, 'sfghhjkd1334' is not as easy on the eye although it could serve the purpose just fine.

EntityID is quite an important element - much like a country code, it can make or break the connection. As such, I often get asked "what happens to the entityID upon switching from one software to another?" The answer is - nothing needs to happen unless you choose so. You may decide to keep it exactly the same and users will not know the difference or change it to match the new software. Changing the entityID will require appropriate notifications sent to your users as well as online content providers.

Ok, last bit. Your population has grown and you now have more than one city. If you are Spain, how do we help route call to Madrid and not Zaragoza? We use a city code or scope "madrid.es". Here's how this would look like in a SAML call directory:

EntityID: https://idp.espana.es/metadata
Scope: madrid.es, zaragoza.es, barcelona.es, valencia.es, seville.es, palma.es
And if you happen to be Monaco?
EntityID: https://idp.monaco.mc/metadata
Scope: monaco.mc

☞ **KEY POINTS**

Identity Provider or IdP creates virtual identities for users. Institutions use various software products for this task: Shibboleth, OpenAthens, ADFS, etc

EntityID uniquely identifies each Identity Provider

Scope is the 'perimeter' of where the user is coming from.
For example: "maincampus.university.com", "overseas.university.com"

... and Them

Service Providers are the other half of the SAML equation. Most commonly you will know them as digital content publishers (IEEE, MAG Online Library, ScienceDirect) but a service provider can be anyone enabling their login with this protocol. Blackboard, Moodle, Canvas, EBSCO Discovery, Alma, Office 365, Lynda.com, Google all support SAML for Single Sign On and authentication purposes.

How do publishers recognise their subscribers? They do this by analysing an attributes statement sent to them by the Identity Provider. This statement, called SAML assertion, contains information about the institution and an individual user, based on what you have decided to release. Consider the following scenario: Anna is a physicist from the USA who will be spending few weeks in Switzerland, collaborating with CERN scientists. In addition to an invitation letter, she must produce evidence of her identity and education to obtain her temporary researcher's pass.

When accessing online resources, authorisation decisions are made in a similar manner: the publisher matches your attributes statement to a certain checklist and if conditions are met, access will be granted. If not - denied.

The below is an excerpt from one such attributes statement :

```xml
<saml:Attribute Name="urn:oid:1.3.6.1.4.1.5923.1.1.1.9"
                NameFormat="urn:oasis:names:tc:SAML:2.0:attrname-format:uri"
                >
                <saml:AttributeValue>member@ps.openathens.net</saml:AttributeValue>
</saml:Attribute>
<saml:Attribute Name="emailAddress"
                NameFormat="urn:oasis:names:tc:SAML:2.0:attrname-format:uri"
                >
                <saml:AttributeValue>kristina.botyriute@eduserv.org.uk</saml:AttributeValue>
</saml:Attribute>
```

This is XML so it doesn't look pretty but I bet you can still make out my work email address and member value for scope "ps.openathens.net" As digital privacy is one of the major concerns today, your IdP software should allow you to fine-tune any user related attributes you wish to release or withhold. Such fine-tuning can help achieve the magic combination of security, anonimity and personalisation all at the same time.

Great! We now know about IdP, SP, entityID, scope and attributes - just understanding this terminology can help look good in a technical conversation. The key to it all however, the glue that makes it all work is the **metadata**. Metadata is information about information. Or data about data. Not just any data though - a decriptive one. Any SAML participant has a metadata file that contains their entityID, scope, attributes, login endpoints and other relevant things. As mentioned before, the key concept of SAML is mutual trust and it can be established by exchanging the metadata.

> ☞ KEY POINTS
>
> **Service Provider** means anyone that relies on SAML attributes statement to make authorisation decisions
>
> **A metadata** is a descriptive file defining each SAML participant and providing the necessary information to establish mutual trust

Federation

A federation is a collective of IdPs and SPs that have agreed to trust each other. Remember the metadata from the previous page? One of the rules that define trust and interaction in the federation is an aggregation of information about all parties into a large XML file. This is where Identity Providers and Service Providers would enlist their metadata files to make the secure communication easier. I have come to think of it as a private scientists' party as most federations were established to unite educational bodies of each country. Each has it's own rules of acceptance: to join The UK Access Management Federation for Education and Research the IdP organisation must be an educational or research body based in the United Kingdom. InCommon accepts members from the US higher education, research organisations, or sponsored partners of higher education members. Most federations have geographical restrictions with OpenAthens currently being the only global federation that is not limited to academic institutions (but we could see that change). At the time of writing there are 51 live federations known to REFEDS - the Research and Education Federations group, with further 16 more in a pilot stage.

Federations vary in size and affordability. For example, membership in UK Federation is free whilst AAF - Australian Access Federation charges $8436 joining fee plus $8581 per annum (Aaf.edu.au, 2017).

Finnish Haka federation comprises of 50 members whilst InCommon in the USA boasts a growing community of 944 participants (Incommon.org, 2017). Due to geographical restrictions however, you may not have much choice unless you live in Texas, USA. Texas has three federations of it's own and is eligible to join InCommon as well as the OpenAthens federation. So why would you want to join a federation? Why not just go ahead and create a bunch of one-to-one connections?

First, this would be too cumbersome for everyone involved. It is much easier for a service provider to retrieve records from a big file on the web (or a local copy of this file - even faster!) than to create an in-house records' system to store each organisation's metadata. Furthermore, such a system would have to be continuously updated in case the Identity Provider chances something - a login point for example. For you as an institution the benefits include having all the information about your providers in one place and security assurances. You can expect a certain standard of service throughout the federation and depending on the IdP software in use, completely eliminate the need to involve your technical staff when enabling access to online resources.

> **KEY POINT** Joining a federation can dramatically reduce the effort required to connect users to your digital subscriptions

PILOT FEDERATIONS

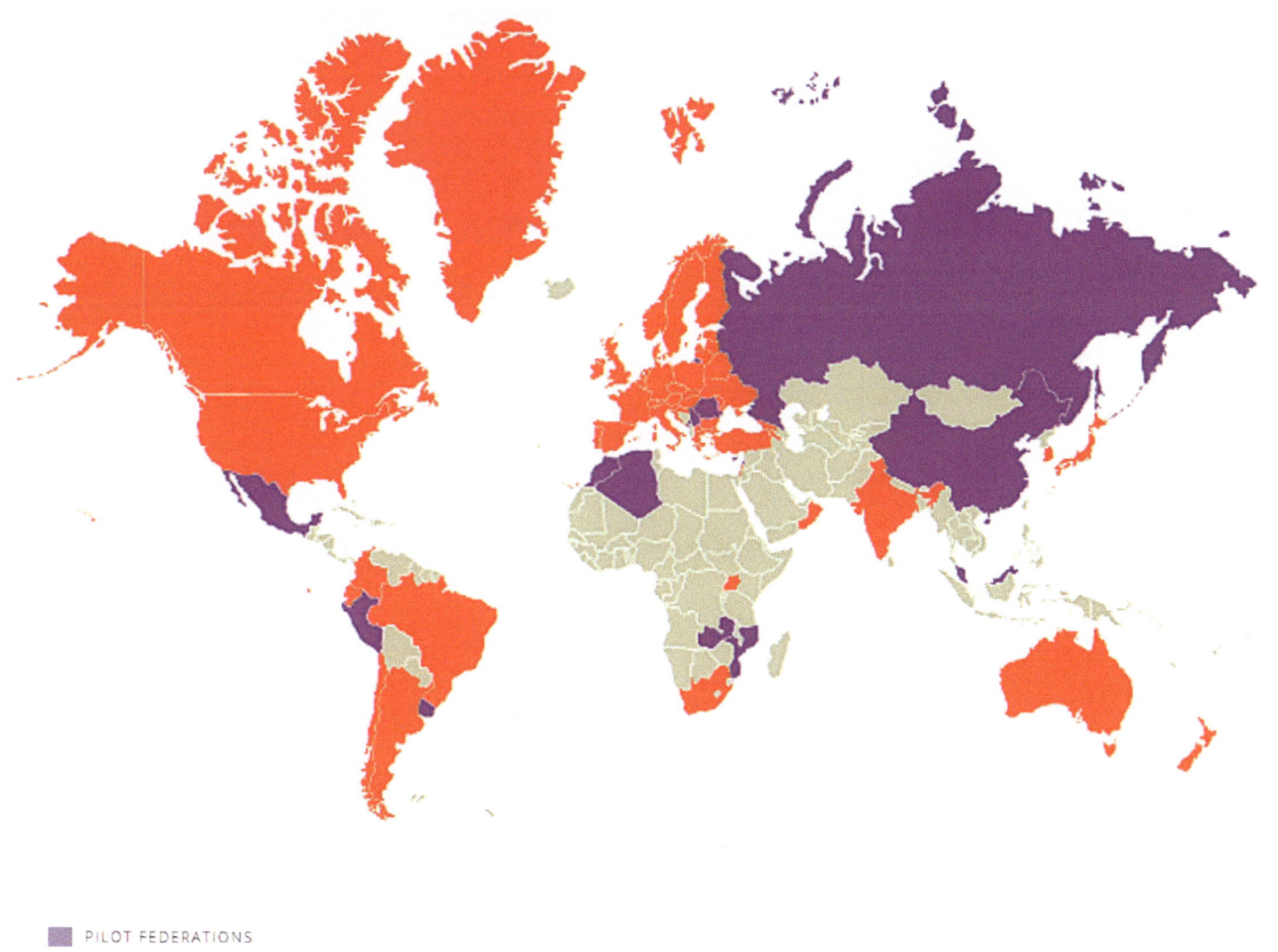

PRODUCTION FEDERATIONS

REFEDS, 2017

Key concepts

SAML
Security Assertion Markup Language. An open standard designed to aid secure Single Sign On

IDENTITY PROVIDER (IDP)
Creates and manages virtual identities

SERVICE PROVIDER (SP)
Makes authorisation decisions based on the SAML attributes statement received from the IdP

ENTITYID
Uniquely identifies SAML participants: SPs and IdPs

SCOPE
Specifies which part of Identity Provider's system the user is coming from

FEDERATION
A collective of IdPs and SPs that trust each other

METADATA
Descriptive data defining every SAML participant

ATTRIBUTES STATEMENT
Selective information about the user IdP releases to SP

OpenID Connect

Open Authorisation 2.0

Open Authorisation (OAuth) is SAML's little sister. It's latest version - OAuth 2.0 was released in May 2010 and is yet to fulfil it's potential though it is fast gaining popularity among mobile application developers. An important observation to make - as the name suggests, OAuth deals with authorisation, not authentication as it is designed to help one application access another application's data.

You may be familiar with this:

Scopus to ORCID	Scopus to ORCID
has asked for the following access to your ORCID record. Add a publication to your publications list. This application will not be able to see your ORCID password, or other private info in your profile. Deny / Authorize	Import your Identifier, profile and publications. The wizard helps you find the correct Scopus profile and to confirm your publications. You can then import the identifier and list of publications into ORCID. Any changes you make will be submitted to the Feedback team to update your Scopus profile. **You will receive this message asking for your authorization to allow Scopus to access your ORCID record. Click on 'Authorize.'**

You may have also seen similar prompts when downloading applications from Google Play or Apple's App Store. As part of the authorisation framework, the application will ask for your permission to access your data from another application. This would sometimes only happen once and other times you would be prompted more frequently.

After clicking 'Authorize' or 'Allow', the app that popped the question will send an **authorisation code** to the app that requested access. In our example it will be ORCID granting access to your data to Scopus. The authorisation code can be compared to a bank cheque - on it's own it's a worthless piece of paper but when you take it to the bank you may exchange it to real money. Some cheques are valid for a month, three or six months but authorisation code's lifetime is normally minutes and seconds. So the receiver must go and cash it in quick to obtain the **access token** (money) in return. This access token will allow it to go to the shop - ORCID - and access information about the user for a certain period of time - ie shop until the money runs out! Sometimes money runs out really quick but some apps are more generous than others and write big cheques. Facebook, for instance, will allow apps to access your data for 60 days.

The process is simple, so not surprisingly the protocol was well-received and quickly adopted. It was soon noticed however that OAuth 2.0 was being misused for authentication which it was never designed to perform. A range of security issues were discovered, most of which are now well documented and available on the World Wide Web. The famous "Signing into One Billion Mobile App Accounts Effortlessly with OAuth 2.0" by Yang, Lau and Liu (2017) is an astonishing example of our incline to trust technology and perhaps a nudge to nurture our inquisitive nature a little bit more.

OpenID Connect

In 2014, a self-proclaimed "league of backstabbing competitors" (Leszcz, 2017) developed OpenID Connect, also known as OIDC - a protocol that adds an authentication layer on top of OAuth 2.0, making it more secure as well as facilitating superior user experience. The protocol was first adopted by it's creators: Google, Microsoft and Ping Identity, then by other technology giants such as Amazon, IBM, ForgeRock and PayPal. Big names sound encouraging but what does it actually do and why would you want to know about it?

Although current library technologies are in no imminent danger to be taken over by OpenID Connect implementations, it is rapidly gaining audience and if all goes well it might just replace SAML in a decade or so. You may already be using applications that promote this authentication method, for example, to access MyDay by Collabco, Moodle, Office365 or Open edX. There is also another reason why I want you to know about OIDC . When choosing between two VLE systems or two student platforms or even between several access options when subscribing to an online resource, the one that supports OpenID Connect should win against the one that only does OAuth, OAuth 1.0 or OAuth 2.0
Even if it's just from security perspective; even if just for you.

Remember the **access token** - real money - that Scopus used to access your data from ORCID? In a scenario where only OAuth 2.0 is used, Scopus has no way of knowing whether you are still logged into ORCID so it can keep on shopping until the money runs out (access token expires). When OpenID Connect is at play however, Scopus would receive an **ID token** together with the access token. In other words, a photocopy of your passport in addition to money. In addition to useful personal information such as name and surname which will help the app provide a better service, the photocopy will contain a time stamp allowing it's validity to expire as well as proof that you are definitely logged in. ID tokens can be signed, encrypted and otherwise secured to a high standard which is another great feature of OpenID Connect.

> ☞ KEY POINTS
>
> **OAuth 2.0** deals with authorisation only, **OpenID Connect** adds an identity layer to it making secure authentication possible.
>
> Think **"app to app"** communication rather than "app to user" or "user to provider". Implementation of this authentication method will normally require some development effort.

Key concepts

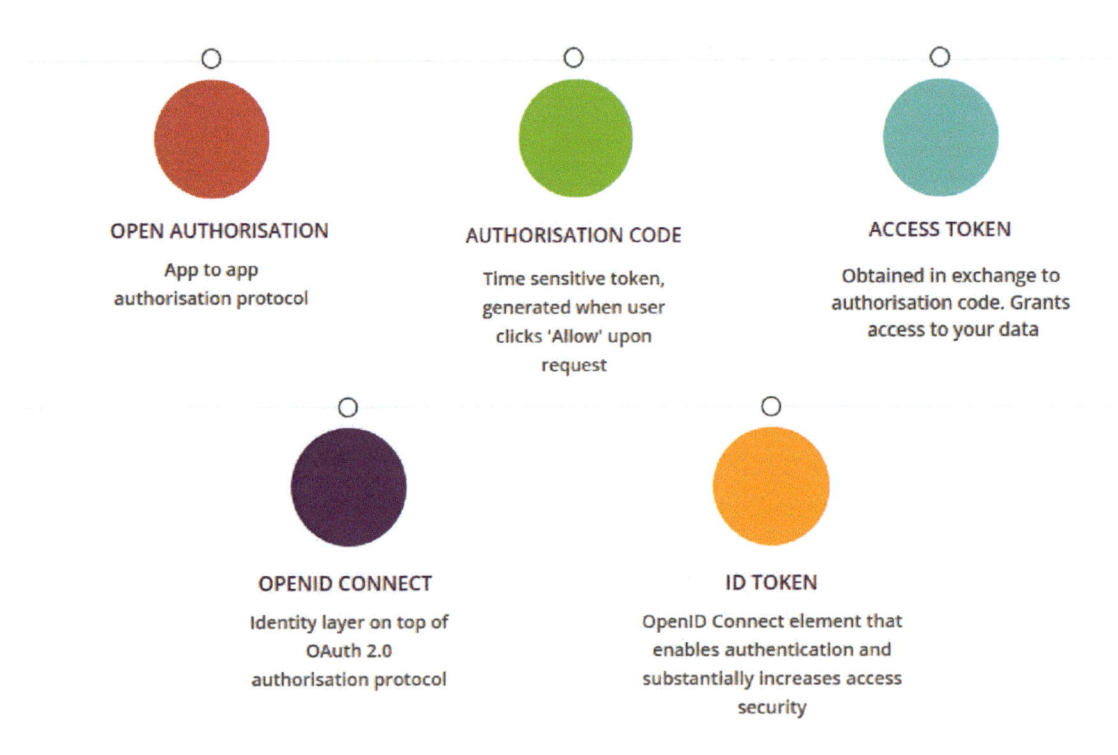

OPEN AUTHORISATION
App to app authorisation protocol

AUTHORISATION CODE
Time sensitive token, generated when user clicks 'Allow' upon request

ACCESS TOKEN
Obtained in exchange to authorisation code. Grants access to your data

OPENID CONNECT
Identity layer on top of OAuth 2.0 authorisation protocol

ID TOKEN
OpenID Connect element that enables authentication and substantially increases access security

Basic Troubleshooting

60 second diagnostics

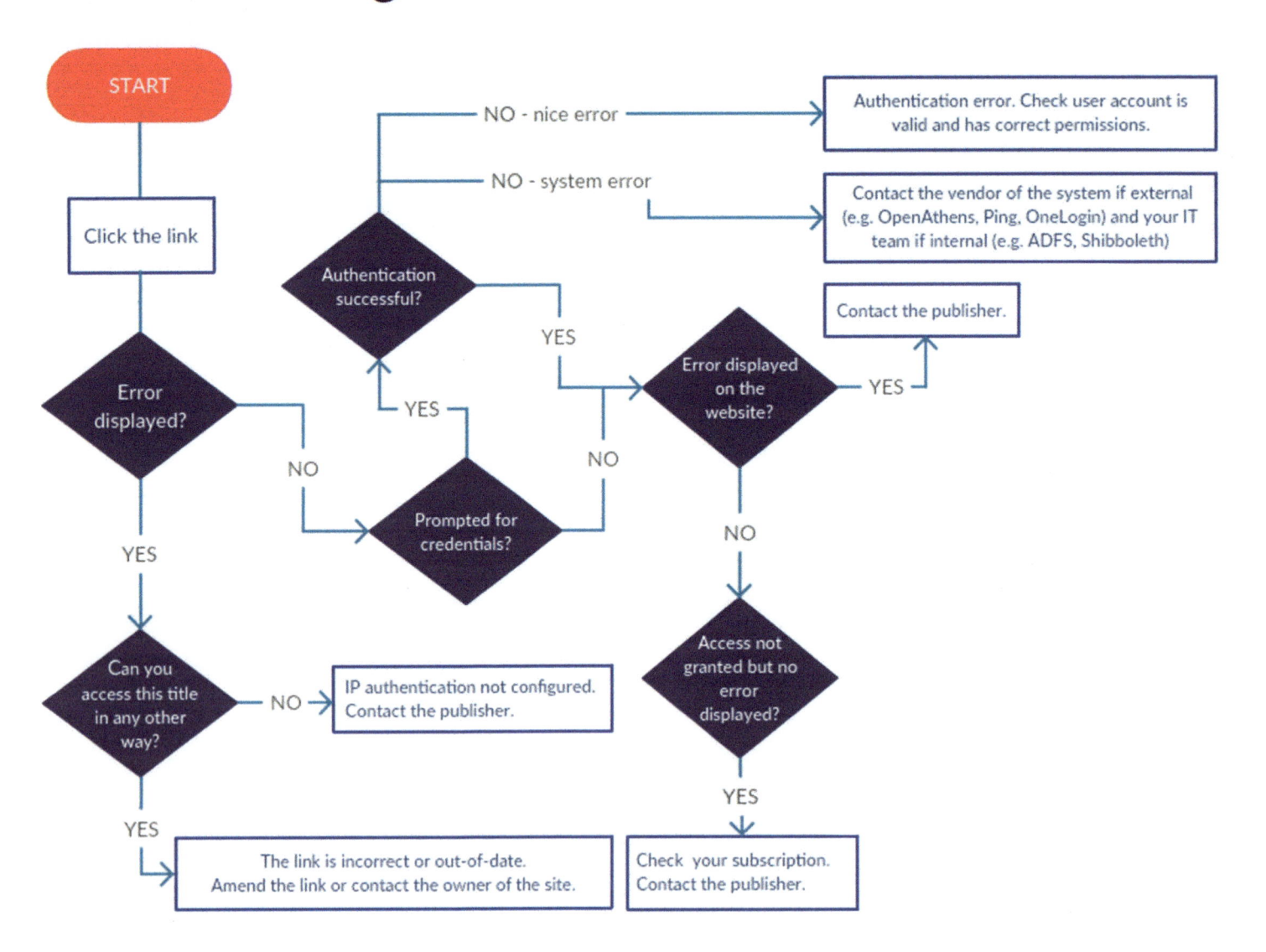

START → Click the link → Error displayed?

- **YES** → Can you access this title in any other way?
  - **NO** → IP authentication not configured. Contact the publisher.
  - **YES** → The link is incorrect or out-of-date. Amend the link or contact the owner of the site.
- **NO** → Prompted for credentials?
  - **YES** → Authentication successful?
    - **NO - nice error** → Authentication error. Check user account is valid and has correct permissions.
    - **NO - system error** → Contact the vendor of the system if external (e.g. OpenAthens, Ping, OneLogin) and your IT team if internal (e.g. ADFS, Shibboleth)
    - **YES** → Error displayed on the website?
      - **YES** → Contact the publisher.
      - **NO** → Access not granted but no error displayed?
        - **YES** → Check your subscription. Contact the publisher.
  - **NO** → (loops to Authentication successful?)

Setting up access

Resource access issues can sometimes be caused by an incomplete setup. If you have used the "60 seconds diagnostics" flowchart and ended up on "Contact the publisher" suggestion, this is probably why. Let's have a look at what providers need from you to successfully enable access for your organisation.

Access by... **username and password.**

Avoid if possible. Nothing is required from you to set this up: the publisher will provide you credentials that you will be asked to share within your institution and users will take it from there.

Access via... **IP recognition.**

Send the publisher the range of your external on-site IP addresses. If you are using proxy to facilitate remote access, add your proxy IP as well, advising that this is a proxy IP (they will see much more traffic from this address and may decide to block it if not notified otherwise). When providing on-site IP addresses, make sure they do not start with 10.*, 172.16.* to 172.31.* or 192.168.* as these addresses are private, meant for internal use only. Your networking team will have set up a translation protocol that turns these internal addresses into one or more external IPs which is what the publisher will be interested in.

Access via... **SAML authentication.**

If your institution belongs to a SAML federation, providers will probably only require your entityID and scope to enable access. Very few would ask for particular attributes - such as email address or a specific string of characters to be passed to them as part of the attributes statement. One thing to bear in mind though (this comes up very often): publishers will often refer to federated access as "Shibboleth". Shibboleth is a popular open source software used to aid SAML authentication which many digital content providers are familiar with. It was so popular in the early days of SAML that the name became synonymous with it and funny enough, some would have never heard of the protocol but would recognize the sound of Shibboleth. Don't let this confuse you - whoever supports Shibboleth will be capable of setting up SAML authentication for you.

If you are looking to make one-to-one SAML connection to an application such as Moodle or Blackboard, instructions will usually be provided. If in doubt, the principle is the same as with the federated access - metadata exchange. You will need to provide your metadata file to the requesting party and obtain theirs, then add theirs to your system and they will add yours.
Job done!

The fastest way to get help

Access disrupted, phone is ringing off the hook while the service desk people on the other end (publisher, software vendor, IT team) are taking their time? Very stressful, very frustrating and it's not your fault! Having had the privilege to be in the role of the outraged customer representing institutional interests as well as a support analyst for such outraged customers I have observed few things that help speed up the resolution time - every time.

1. Try to identify the root cause of the issue if at all possible. Use the flowchart from "60 seconds diagnostics" to get an idea of what may have gone wrong. This step will either save you a lot of time or at the very least reduce the likelihood of hearing it's someone else's problem.

2. Pick up the phone. Really. This is an obvious one but you would be surprised how rarely people do it! If you are looking for quick results, opt for a call rather than email. I will agree with you if you have just thought to yourself it is impossible to find online publisher's help desk numbers. Online forms and email addresses that send automatic "we will get back to you within the next 24 hours to 5 working days" replies makes their life easier, helps manage the workload and so on. However if your institution has got an audit in the next few hours or access to the resource you have based your presentation on is not working... I call it mission critical.

Can't find the number for the help desk? Call their sales team or if you have one - your sales representative. I **guarantee** they will pass you through to the technical team or get them to call you back. (Sound distressed!)

3. Email screenshots and steps to reproduce the issue. This is just as essential as getting help desk's attention in the first place. Unless you are affected by a service-wide issue or it's a well-known bug, the technical team will not know precisely what is wrong. One thing I have learnt is that there are million ways to get to the same error message. Tell them exactly what you clicked on, where it took you and attach the screenshot of the error message that followed. If at all possible, provide test credentials.

4. Confirm the person dealing with your issue. A name and help desk's number is a great start - sometimes just knowing your special helper's name inspires greater responsibility. If all else fails, you can at least encourage accountability.

On the other end of the scale are super-helpful workers who will not hesitate to provide you with their personal work email address or direct dial. This is amazing when dealing with an ongoing emergency, however if you want this special attention when the next disaster strikes, better not put the poor guy on speed dial for not so urgent issues.

The End

You've made it!
I sincerely thank you for your time.
The world of identity and access management is vast and growing fast but so little of it affects how we access online resources today.
I am excited to see new technologies seep into the library and enrich the way people experience knowledge.

With promising projects well under way we may finally be able to combine security with usability.
Librarians are getting very savvy working with all the different, sometimes even incompatible, systems they are presented with. I hope this won't be necessary for long.

Lastly, I hope this short read will have made your access management less of a maze and more a walk in the park.

Yours truly,

Kristina

Bibliography

Aaf.edu.au. (2017). Australian Access Federation. [online] Available at: https://aaf.edu.au/price [Accessed 10 Jul. 2017].

Edgar, L. (2015). EZproxy: Migrating From a Local Server to a Hosted Environment. Journal of Electronic Resources Librarianship, 27(3), pp.194-199.

Fontana, J. (2017). Hacks battered IT optimism in 2016; can 2017 enrich defenses | ZDNet. [online] ZDNet. Available at: http://www.zdnet.com/article/hacks-battered-it-optimism-in-2016-can-2017-enrich-defenses [Accessed 9 Jul. 2017].

Ft.com. (2017). Financial Times. [online] Available at: https://ft.com [Accessed 9 Jul. 2017].

Gartner IT Glossary. (2017). Identity Management - Access Management - Gartner Research. [online] Available at: https://research.gartner.com/definition-whatis-identity-access-management [Accessed 11 Jul. 2017].

Incommon.org. (2017). InCommon Participants. [online] Available at: https://www.incommon.org/participants [Accessed 10 Jul. 2017].

Leach, P., Franks, J., Luotonen, A., Hallam-Baker, P., Lawrence, S., Hostetler, J. and Stewart, L. (2017). RFC 2617 - HTTP Authentication: Basic and Digest Access Authentication. [online] Tools.ietf.org. Available at: https://tools.ietf.org/html/rfc2617 [Accessed 11 Jul. 2017].

Leach, P., Franks, J., Luotonen, A., Hallam-Baker, P., Lawrence, S., Hostetler, J. and Stewart, L. (2017). RFC 2617 - HTTP Authentication: Basic and Digest Access Authentication. [online] Tools.ietf.org. Available at: https://tools.ietf.org/html/rfc2617 [Accessed 11 Jul. 2017].

Leszcz, M. (2017). The Foundation of Internet Identity | OpenID. [online] Openid.net. Available at: http://openid.net/2016/09/27/the-foundation-of-internet-identity [Accessed 11 Jul. 2017].

Publisher Solutions International (2017). The IP Registry - The Global IP Address Database. [online] Theipregistry.org. Available at: http://theipregistry.org [Accessed 11 Jul. 2017].

REFEDS (2017). Federations Map. [image] Available at: https://refeds.org/federations/federations-map [Accessed 11 Jul. 2017].

Winnard, K., Bussche, M., Choi, W. and Rossi, D. (2016). Managing Digital Certificates across the Enterprise. [S.l.]: IBM Redbooks, p.16.

Wright, C., Freedman, B. and Liu, D. (2008). The IT regulatory and standards compliance handbook. Burlington, MA: Syngress Pub., pp.522-523.

Yang, R., Lau, W. and Liu, T. (2017). Signing into One Billion Mobile App Accounts Effortlessly with OAuth2.0. [ebook] Available at: https://www.blackhat.com/docs/eu-16/materials/eu-16-Yang-Signing-Into-Billion-Mobile-Apps-Effortlessly-With-OAuth20-wp.pdf [Accessed 11 Jul. 2017].

Open Access This book is licensed under the terms of the Creative Commons Attribution 4.0 International License (http://creativecommons.org/licenses/by/4.0/), which permits use, sharing, adaptation, distribution and reproduction in any medium or format, as long as you give appropriate credit to the original author(s) and the source, provide a link to the Creative Commons license and indicate if changes were made.

The images or other third party material in this book are included in the book's Creative Commons license, unless indicated otherwise in a credit line to the material. If material is not included in the book's Creative Commons license and your intended use is not permitted by statutory regulation or exceeds the permitted use, you will need to obtain permission directly from the copyright holder.